We Like To Read

D1309284

We Like to Read

ELYSE APRIL

Illustrations by
Angie Thompson

HOHM PRESS
Prescott, Arizona

For Lee, for Aaron and for children everywhere.

Cover design, interior layout and design: Zac Parker, Kadak Graphics, Prescott, AZ.

Library of Congress Cataloging in Publication Data:

April, Elyse.
 We like to read : a picture book for pre-readers & parents / Elyse April ; illustrations by Angie Thompson.
     p. cm.
 ISBN-13: 978-1-890772-80-2 (trade pbk. : alk. paper)
 ISBN-10: 1-890772-80-1 (trade pbk. : alk. paper)
 1. Books and reading--Juvenile literature. I. Thompson, Angie, ill. II. Title.
 Z1003.A67 2008
 028.5'5--dc22
                         2007041967

HOHM PRESS
P.O. Box 2501
Prescott, AZ 86302
800-381-2700
http://www.hohmpress.com

This book was printed in China.
Cover Illustration: Angie Thompson

PREFACE

Reading can be one of life's greatest joys and the foundation for all learning. The preparation for reading includes subtle communication skills of mood and gesture, tone and syntax. By relating to our children as the active bodies, minds and hearts that they are – ready to absorb knowledge, even in utero – we are respecting their innate intelligence, and providing them with the keys to becoming full adult human beings.

WE LIKE TO READ is based on the author's twelve years as an early childhood educator in a community setting, supplemented by research provided in *Language and Literacy: Supports for Struggling Readers: Meeting the Goals of No Child Left Behind* by Renitta Goldman, Jerry Alderidge and Kelly A. Russell (Birmingham, Alabama: Seacoast Publishing, 2007).

The bright and engaging pictures in *WE LIKE TO READ* provide cues for parents and caretakers of young children to enhance children's readiness for reading. As opposed to force-feeding information and exerting pressure to achieve, *WE LIKE TO READ* promotes a holistic approach, involving all of the senses and encouraging children to simply PLAY!

Enjoy this book with your children and grow a garden of fervent readers.

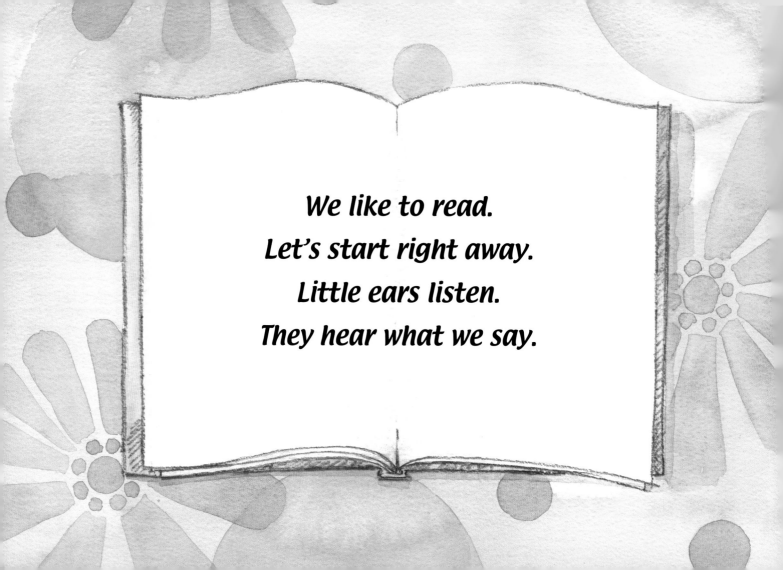

We like to read.
Let's start right away.
Little ears listen.
They hear what we say.

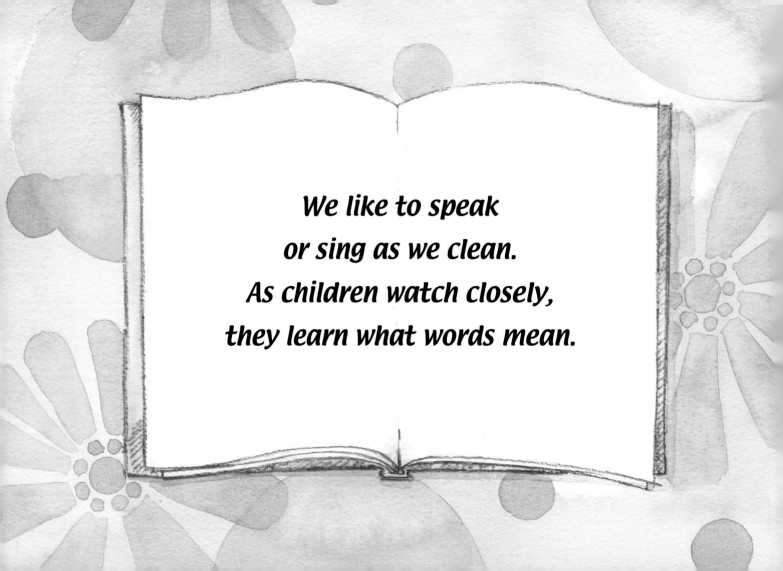

We like to speak
or sing as we clean.
As children watch closely,
they learn what words mean.

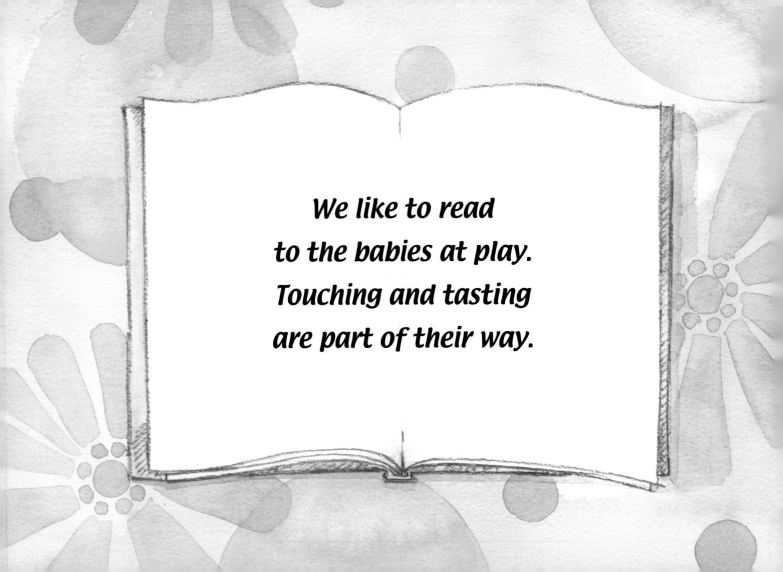

We like to read
to the babies at play.
Touching and tasting
are part of their way.

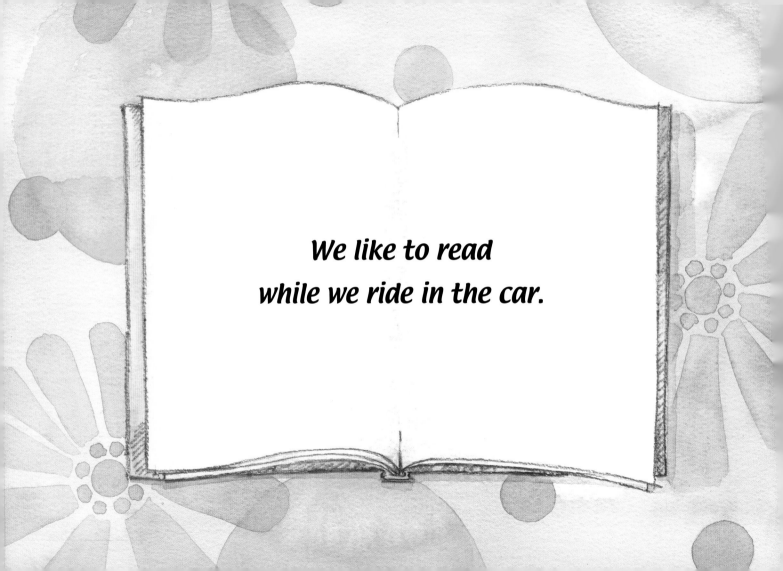

We like to read
while we ride in the car.

A trip to the library
is never too far.

*We like to write
and scribble and draw.*

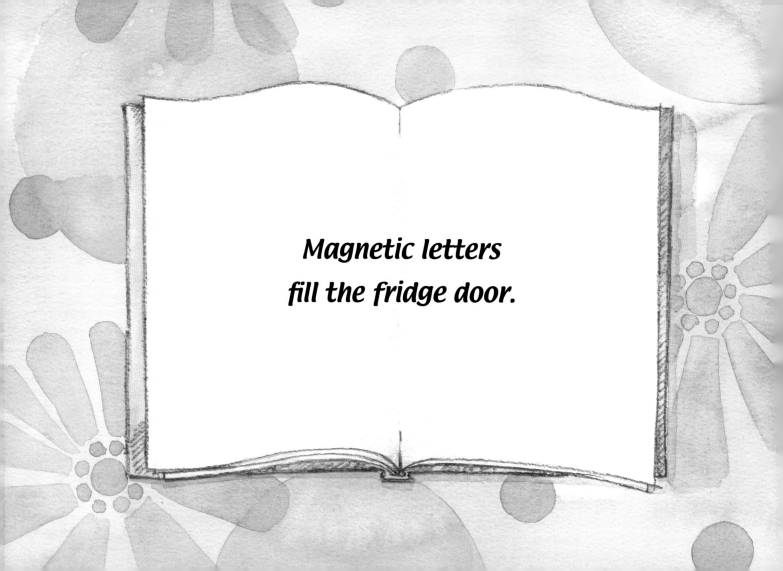

Magnetic letters
fill the fridge door.

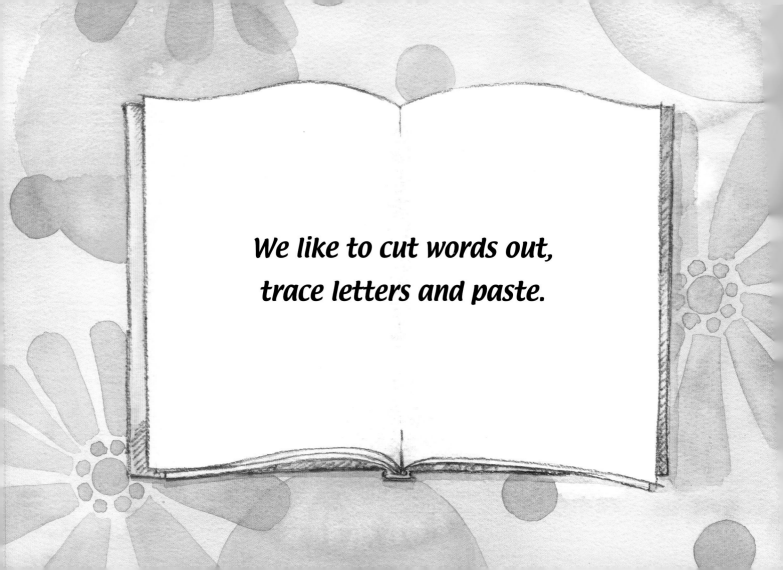

We like to cut words out,
trace letters and paste.

*We label our toys
and put each in its place.*

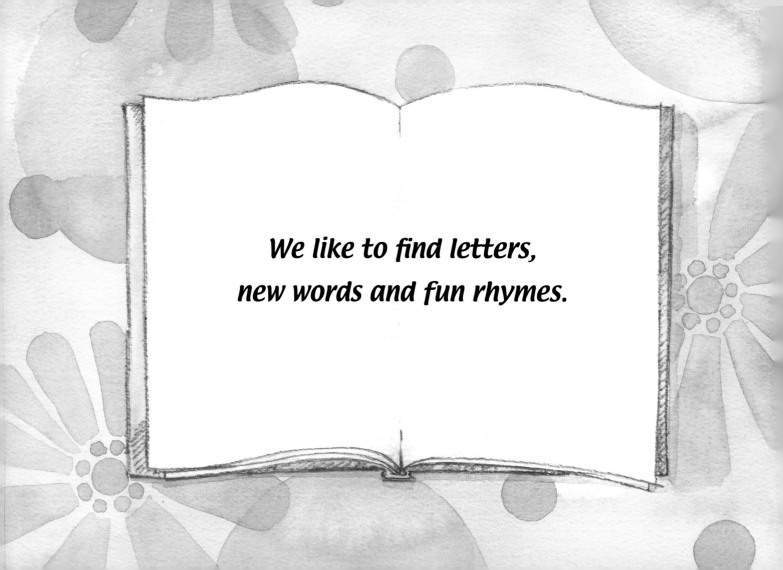

We like to find letters,
new words and fun rhymes.

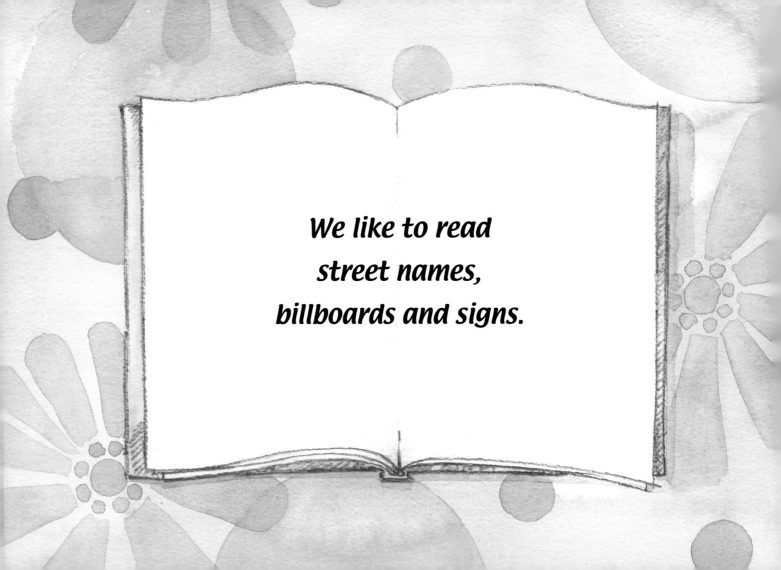

We like to read
street names,
billboards and signs.

We like to tell stories,
dress up and record.
Books are good friends
and we never get bored.

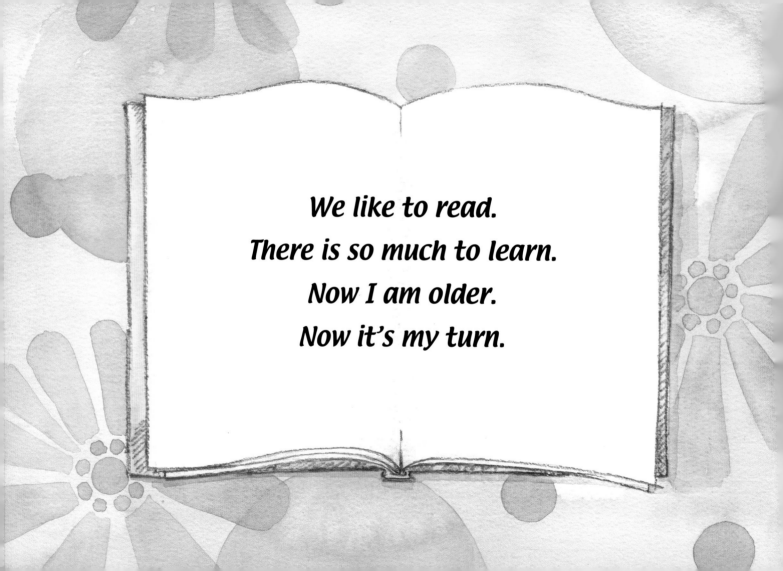

We like to read.

There is so much to learn.

Now I am older.

Now it's my turn.

OTHER FAMILY HEALTH TITLES FROM HOHM PRESS

We Like To Nurse
by Chia Martin
Illustrations by Shukyo Rainey
Captivating illustrations present mother animals nursing their young, and honors the mother-child bond created by nursing. (Ages: Infants and up)
ISBN: 978-934252-45-4, paper, 32 pages, $9.95
Spanish Language Version: *Nos Gusta Amamanatar*
ISBN: 978-890772-41-3

We Like To Help Cook
by Marcus Allsop
Illustrations by Diane Iverson
Based on the USDA Food Pyramid guidelines, young children help adults to prepare healthy, delicious foods. (Ages: 2-6)
ISBN: 978-890772-70-3, paper, 32 pages, $9.95
Spanish Language Version: *Nos Gusta Ayudar a Cocinar*
ISBN: 978-1-890772-75-8

We Like To Move: Exercise Is Fun
by Elyse April
Illustrations by Diane Iverson
This vividly-colored picture book encourages exercise as a prescription against obesity and diabetes in young children. (Ages: Infants-6)
ISBN: 978-890772-60-4, paper, 32 pages, $9.95
Spanish Language Version: *Nos Gusta Movernos: El Ejercicio Es Divertido* ISBN: 978-890772-65-9

We Like To Eat Well
by Elyse April
Illustrations by Lewis Agrell
This book celebrates healthy food, and encourages young children and their caregivers to eat well, and with greater awareness. (Ages: Infants-6)
ISBN: 978-890772-69-7, paper, 32 pages, $9.95
Spanish Language Version: *Nos Gusta Comer Bien*
ISBN: 978-1-890772-78-9

TO ORDER: *800-381-2700, or visit our website, www.hohmpress.com *Special discounts for bulk orders.*